Going
to the
Beach

Written by Jo S. Kittinger
Illustrated by Shari Warren

Children's Press®
A Division of Scholastic Inc.
New York • Toronto • London • Auckland • Sydney
Mexico City • New Delhi • Hong Kong
Danbury, Connecticut

For Larry Dane Brimner, with thanks
—J.S.K.

To my daughter, Alexandra, who loves the beach
and made sure all the illustrations in this story
passed the "kid-test"
—S.W.

Reading Consultants

Linda Cornwell
Literacy Specialist

Katharine A. Kane
Education Consultant
(Retired, San Diego County Office of Education and
San Diego State University)

Library of Congress Cataloging-in-Publication Data

Kittinger, Jo S.
  Going to the beach / written by Jo S. Kittinger : illustrated by Shari Warren.
    p. cm. — (Rookie reader)
  Summary: A family spends a day at the beach enjoying the water, sand, and sun.
  ISBN 0-516-22535-9 (lib. bdg.)   0-516-27370-1 (pbk.)
  [1. Beaches—Fiction.] I. Warren, Shari, ill. II. Title. III. Series.
  PZ7.K67152 Go 2002
  [E]—dc21   2001008378

CHILDREN'S PRESS, AND A ROOKIE READER®, and associated logos are trademarks and or
registered trademarks of Grolier Publishing Co., Inc. SCHOLASTIC and
associated logos are trademarks and or registered trademarks of Scholastic Inc.
1 2 3 4 5 6 7 8 9 10 R 11 10 09 08 07 06 05 04 03 02

Grab your goggles.

3

Pack your pail.

We're going to the beach.

Find your flip-flops.
Take your towel.

We're going to the beach!

The sand is hot.
The water is cool.

Splash!
Swish!
Catch a fish!

Dive.
Float.
Bail the boat.

Make a castle.
Jump the foam.

Shake out sand.

We're going home.

Word List (35 words)

a	dive	going	out	take
bail	find	grab	pack	the
beach	fish	home	pail	to
boat	flip-flops	hot	sand	towel
castle	float	is	shake	water
catch	foam	jump	splash	we're
cool	goggles	make	swish	your

About the Author

Jo S. Kittinger, a native of Florida, lived in several states before settling in Alabama. A love of books and a passion to create inspire Jo to write both fiction and nonfiction books for children. While teaching her own children to read, Jo realized the critical role of emergent readers. Jo enjoys pottery, photography, and reading in her spare time. Going to the beach usually means a visit to her mother, who lives just ten minutes from the white sands of the Gulf of Mexico.

About the Illustrator

Shari Warren was born to draw. Ever since she was old enough to hold a crayon, she was drawing everything she could see and think—from her brother's funny toes to the monsters in her closet. She especially enjoyed drawing people and making up stories to go along with her pictures. Her professional career has spanned the publishing and entertainment industry, yet creating art and stories for children is her passion.

Shari lives in the San Francisco Bay Area with her husband, Michael (her greatest love), her daughter Alexandra (her greatest joy), and her doggie Maxine (her greatest fan).